HOW COME
I'VE NEVER
SEEN
A CAN OF
BROCCOLI?

HOW COME I'VE NEVER SEEN A CAN OF BROCCOLI?

Brian & Meghan Black

Aivilo Press / 2001

Design by Dennis Kashton

National Library of Canada Cataloguing in Publication Data

Black, Brian, 1947
  How come I've never seen a can of broccoli?

ISBN 0-9686942-1-7

I.Canadian wit and humour(English)* I.Black,Meghan,1980- II.
Title.
PS8553.L3182H68 2001   C818.602   C2001-911528-8
PR9199.4.B52H68 2001

Introduction

Most of the more than 200 observations of our
everyday lives listed in this book are original. Others,
we have borrowed from writings, heard or have been
suggested by many friends over the years.

We thought it might be fun to list these musings under
the title "How Come I've Never Seen a Can of
Broccoli?"

We enjoyed putting these together and we hope you
will enjoy them also.

Brian & Meghan Black

TABLE OF CONTENTS

CHURCH

If there is a best man at every wedding, how come we don't marry him?

How come a marriage license is the only license that does not expire?

How come saints only have first names?

If an annulment means the wedding never took place, what was everyone doing that day?

If we marry the whole person, how come we only ask for their hand in marriage?

If God created Adam and Eve, how come they have belly buttons?

If God created the universe, what was he doing the day before?

How do we really know that all those people in the obituary column passed away "peacefully"?

If man evolved from monkeys and apes, how come we still have monkeys and apes?

How come the obituary section of a newspaper is in the "Life And Entertainment" section?

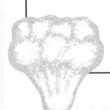

If you are a Christian, do you ever wonder how 8 million Hindus can be wrong?

If someone passes away at one hundred years of age, how come we say they died suddenly?

If Christ was crucified, how come we call it Good Friday?

How come we nail down the lid of a coffin?

SHOPPING

If 7-Eleven convenience stores are open **24** hours a day, how come there are locks on the door?

If all plants and animals come from seeds, where do seedless grapes come from?

If it is good to the very last drop, what is wrong with the last drop?

How come evaporated milk does not disappear?

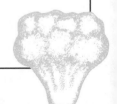

Who is the whiz that spelled cheese "cheez"?

How come we do not ask what the other 98% is in 2% milk?

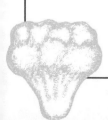

If it's evaporated milk why is there still milk in the can?

How come children's cough medicine has the warning "do not drive or operate machinery"?

How come sleep medication says that it may cause drowsiness?

How come there is an expiration date on sour cream?

If you remove the bones from fish how come it's called "boned"?

If they are called shelled peanuts, how come there's no shell?

How come a pineapple is the only apple that doesn't grow on a tree?

How come I can't pull a shirt, with a neck size 16 over my size 7 hat?

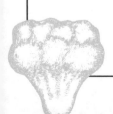

If it is made in England how come we call it China?

How can all the new books in the bookstore be the bestseller?

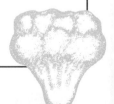

If my suit size if 38 and my wife's suit size is 12, how come I'm not at least three times larger than my wife?

How come umbrellas have a handle right in the middle where you want to stand when it's raining?

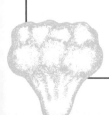

If hotdogs are sold in packages of 12, how come the buns are sold in packages of 8?

How come pharmacists work on raised platforms?

How come there are no bumble berries in Bumbleberry Pie?

How come I've never been able to find Chanel No.1?

How can you sell donut holes?

How can a sauce be sweet and sour at the same time?

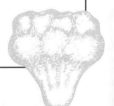

If the legal age for buying cigarettes is eighteen, how come that sign says they will check I.D. if you look <u>twenty-five</u> or younger?

How come I've never been able to find Preparation A through G?

How come lemon juice contains mostly artificial ingredients but dishwashing liquid contains <u>real</u> lemons?

How come shelled peanuts have shells?

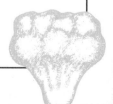

How come boned chicken doesn't have any bones?

How come the nozzle connection on a propane tank is always tightened counter-clockwise?

How come the balm for chapped lips is spelled **<u>LYP</u>**?

If you are on an escalator going up, how do you push the emergency button to stop at the bottom of the escalator?

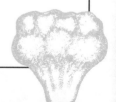

How come pitted plums don't have pits?

How come publishers write inside their newest novel "available wherever books are sold"?

How come a dozen brown eggs are more expensive than a dozen white eggs?

SPORTS

If we are already there, how come we all sing "Take me out to the ball game"?

How come we all "sit" in the stands?

How come track events always run in a counter-clockwise direction?

If the first point in tennis is 15, the second point 30, how come the third point is 40?

How come baseball umps always turn around to clean home plate?

How come the batting instructor, who knows everything about hitting, is not in the lineup?

How come baseball is the only sport where the manager wears a uniform?

If Montreal was the first professional hockey team, whom did they play?

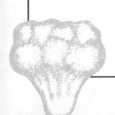

How come baseball hats have that
little button at the top of the cap?

If all kick-offs in football are onside
how come we only call the ten yarder
an onside kick?

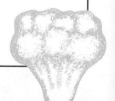

If a celebrity at the baseball game throws <u>out</u> the first pitch how come he doesn't throw it to second base?

How come golf caddies at the Masters wear the same coveralls as mechanics?

How come a boxing <u>ring</u> is square?

How come basketball is the only sport where music is allowed during play?

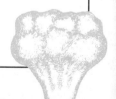

TRAVEL

How come there are interstate highways in Hawaii?

How come we drive on parkways and park on driveways?

How come they call it rush hour when your car is standing still in traffic?

How come there's no apostrophe in the **DONT WALK** light?

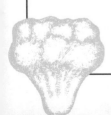

How can you get where you are going
if you are on a "non-stop" flight?

How come we pay money to drive
on a freeway?

How come, after you go through airport security, the people in first class get real knives with serrated edges?

How come we push harder on the remote button when we know the battery is dead?

If two airplanes almost collide, how come we call it a near <u>miss</u>?

How come we put suits in a garment bag and garments in a suitcase?

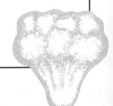

How come in hotels I've never seen anyone sitting on those chairs at either end of the mirror opposite the elevator on every floor?

How come a man's bicycle has a high crossbar?

How come reverse is ahead of forward on an automatic transmission?

If you give birth while flying over the Atlantic what should you write for country of birth?

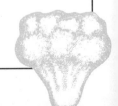

If Avis has been trying harder for so many years how come they aren't No.1 by now?

If you're in your car traveling at the speed of light what happens if you turn on your headlights?

How come you lock your luggage if it's stored in the belly of the aircraft at 37,000 feet?

When NASA sends up a space shuttle where does the shuttle occur?

If its fluorescent orange how come we call it the black box?

If the speed limit is 50 mph in the city and 80 mph outside the city, how come we don't just post one sign saying you are leaving the city?

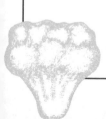

How come when I drive through a yellow traffic light and look in my rear view mirror, I see at least three more cars come through the intersection?

If you wear rubber boots while visiting an English farm, how come you have to step in the disinfectant in your regular shoes when you return?

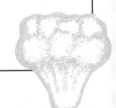

If it's called a "touchless" car wash, how come we lower the antenna?

If we are driving and looking for an address, how come we turn down the volume on the radio?

How come I've never seen deer crossing at that yellow road sign?

If you have plastic surgery in another country, how can you use the same passport photo on your return?

How come only one mirror has that sign "objects are closer than they appear"?

HOME

If nothing sticks to Teflon how does it stick to the frying pan?

How come we say the alarm clock goes <u>off</u>?

If you only get one, how come they call it a television set?

If father knows best, why ask anyone else?

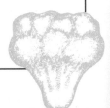

If my shoe size is nine, how come I buy socks size $9\frac{1}{2}$ - 11?

How come tubs and bathroom sinks have overflow outlets while kitchen sinks do not?

How come there are no **A** or **B** batteries? (Just **AA**, **AAA**, **C**, **D**, etc.)

How come a garage is never for sale at a "garage sale"?

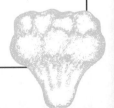

How come mattresses all have floral designs on them?

If we have already washed ourselves clean how come we wash the bath towels?

How can you tell if you are out of invisible ink?

If it is a circular drive how do you get out?

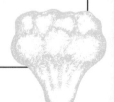

How do "Don't walk on the grass" signs get there?

How would I know if a word in the dictionary was misspelled?

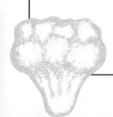

How do we know that the new dog food has an improved taste?

How come glue doesn't stick to the inside of the bottle?

How come no one can explain the difference between heating the oven and pre-heating the oven?

How come they are called apartments if they are all joined together?

If we demolish a building by knocking it down, how come we call it a razing?

How come there are different colored bristles on a toothbrush?

If you mail a letter to the post office how does it get delivered?

How come you start at the top when buttoning a button-<u>up</u> sweater?

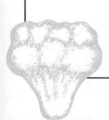

If the census form is confidential how do they know whom to penalize if you refuse to fill it out?

How come men's pajamas have those little breast pockets?

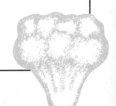

If the T.V. advertisement tells you that you need this product without delay how come it takes six to eight weeks for it to arrive?

If you are bald, how do you fill in the section of your driver's license asking for hair colour?

If you are supposed to pull the toilet paper from underneath, how come the flowers are on the outside of the roll?

If you want to close down your computer, how come you click on "start"?

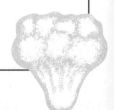

MISCELLANEOUS

If we are learning by "phonetics", how come it is not spelled with an "F"?

How come "slim" chance and "fat" chance mean the same thing?

If you win automatically why do you have to answer a skill-testing question?

How come no matter what I am wearing, belly button lint is always grayish blue in color?

How come the donut lady uses those little wax papers to put your donuts in the bag and then puts the paper in the bag with the donuts?

If we grade papers A to F, how come there is no E?

If my hat size is 8 and my neck size is 16, how come my neck is not twice the size of my head?

If Barbie is so popular how come you have to buy her friends?

How come a 14 year old pays the adult price for a movie but can't go and see an adult movie?

What do we call an elevator when it's going down?

How come we call it the "shoulder" blade if it's on our back?

If a dog has only two puppies how come we don't call them twins?

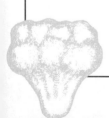

How come little safety pins are gold
and the bigger ones are silver?

How come we say, "the truth of the
rumor is"?

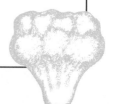

How come phone-in psychics have to ask what your name is?

How come we prep the IV site prior to a lethal injection?

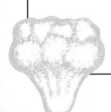

If it says Large Animal Hospital does that mean the hospital or the animals are large?

If all animals only see black and white, how come we use a red cape while fighting a bull?

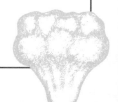

How come we say "a new tradition"?

If Superman is so clever how come he wears his underwear on the outside?

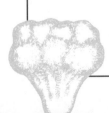

How come Scotland Yard is in London?

How come we call it a Civil War?

If they are already finished how come
we call them buildings?

How come we all have to touch the
door with the wet paint sign?

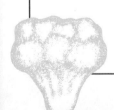

How come we say your feet smell and your nose runs?

How come we call them walking shoes?

How come I've never seen a flag fly?

How can you stand on your head?

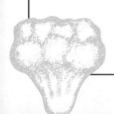

If we put our shirts and trousers on them should we still call them "coat hangers"?

How come kamikaze pilots wear helmets?

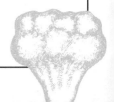

If the rain keeps up, do we all stay dry?

How old is an artifact dated 5000 years B.C. to an atheist?

How come we turn the page of a newspaper from the bottom and a paperback from the top?

If the problem is in the stomach, how come we call it "heart burn"?

If there is a Third World how come I can't name the second?

If no one weighs himself or herself before getting on the elevator how do we know if we reached the limit?

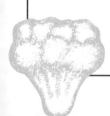

If they never post or mail anything, how come we call them postmen and mailmen?

If putting people in one room is supposed to encourage people to talk, how come nobody talks in an elevator?

How can you sit <u>in</u> a chair?

How come I've never seen a baby pigeon?

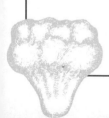

What valley do those lilies come from anyway?

How come bi-weekly and bi-monthly mean the same thing?

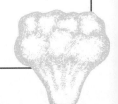

How come inflammable and flammable mean the same thing?

How come people always push the elevator button when it's already lit?

If nothing in life is free, how come we all get free advice?

How come I've never seen the homeless in the country?

How come Tarzan doesn't have a beard?

How come there is no East Virginia?

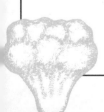

How come pirates wear earrings?

If there are no survivors how come
we send in <u>rescue</u> workers?

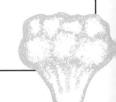

If it is going down, do the Brits still call it a "lift"?

How come no one works on Labor Day?

What color do traffic lights appear to people who are colorblind?

How come abbreviated is such a long word?

If its zero degrees outside today and its supposed to be twice as cold tomorrow how cold will it be?

Do skydivers ever use that expression "If at first you don't succeed"?

How come if you deliver something by car it's called a "shipment" and if you deliver something by ship its called "cargo"?

How come no one has ever forgotten how to ride a bicycle?

How come banks charge you a "non-sufficient funds" fee on money they already know you don't have?

How come there are five syllables in the word "monosyllabic"?

If there is a forty percent chance of showers, and it's raining, why don't they change the percentage to one hundred?

If a same sex couple adopts a child, how do they decide what the last name should be?

How come I've never seen "Dad"
tattooed on anyone?

How come some envelopes show
you where to place the stamp?

How come some electric fans have those little paper streamers tied to the grill?

If you are an assistant professor which professor are you helping?

If you have been told to remain silent, how do you call your lawyer?

Do people in Tipperary ever sing that song?

If you push back a date, how come you move it ahead?

How come I've never seen wings on a buffalo?

How come no one can tell me how many days there are in a week and a half?

If dogs don't like you blowing in their faces, how come the first thing they do in the car is stick their heads out the window?

How come they have Braille on the ATM machine at the drive through window?

How come you can't tickle yourself?

How come there is no **Z** on a touch tone telephone?

If you've lost something how come everyone asks "Where did you leave it"?